Phlegal

H/6

THE MEDIEVAL TOWN

THEN AND THERE SERIES

GENERAL EDITOR

MARJORIE REEVES, M.A., Ph.D.

The Medieval Town

MARJORIE REEVES, M.A., Ph.D.

Illustrated from contemporary sources by

F. E. GORNIOT

LONGMANS

LONGMANS, GREEN AND CO. LTD
48 Grosvenor Street, London W.1

Associated companies, branches and representatives
throughout the world

First published 1954
Seventh impression 1964
Eighth impression 1966
Ninth impression 1968

Printed in Hong Kong by Peninsula Press Ltd.

CONTENTS

TO THE READER

EVERY fact in this book comes from some record written at the time the book is describing; nothing has been invented in these pages, which seek to be a true record of the life and thought of people who themselves lived in a medieval town. What they wrote are original sources to which historians have to go back for their information. If you want to write a historical play or novel, see if you too can take all your detail exactly and accurately from original sources.

In the same way some of the pictures in this book are based on a drawing made by someone who lived then and there. You will find out more about these original sources and pictures by reading pages 81 and 82.

By studying what people said in word and picture about themselves, you will come to feel at home in one 'patch' of the history of the past and really live with the group of people as they thought and worked then and there. And gradually you will be able to fill in more patches of history.

The Editors acknowledge with thanks the help and advice given by Mr. Edward R. Thomas, M.A., B.SC., in preparing this book.

THIS BOOK IS ABOUT A TOWN AND THE MEN WHO MADE IT

Do YOU live in a great city, a small country town or a village ? Wherever it is, almost certainly you live in a place that was made by other people before you. As you walk through the streets you can ask yourself : ' Who were the people who made this place what it is to-day ? ' I wonder what you would think if one of them suddenly came walking towards you down the road ? Would you just stop and stare or would you want to ask him lots of questions ?

This book is about an old town—Salisbury—and the men who made it. Here you can ask these men questions. You can find out how they worked and how they played 500 years ago. Perhaps the people who made your town did very much the same sort of things, so that finding out about Salisbury may answer some of the questions about your own home. But go on asking your questions ! Find out all you can about your own village or town. Find what it was like 500 years ago and discuss together how far these people who made our towns lived as we do, and how far they did things quite differently.

I

HOW SALISBURY BEGAN

HAVE you ever stopped to ask how towns began in this country ? Our ancestors, the Anglo-Saxons, seem to have been countryfolk rather than townsfolk, and for hundreds of years England was full of villages. There were very few places that WE should have called towns. But the Anglo-Saxons themselves used the word ' town ' (or ' tun ' or ' ton ') for their little villages. How many places do you know which end in ' ton ' ? All these probably began as Anglo-Saxon villages.

But why did people start making towns ? Stop a moment and ask yourself why people live in towns to-day. That's a big question. It would be interesting to discover for yourself all the different reasons which bring people to live in towns now. But away back before 1066 there were no factories, shops or cinemas, so why should people begin living close together in one place ? After all, there was plenty of room in the country, more food, and far less danger of fire than if you huddled all your little wooden houses together in a town. So what made people build towns ?

One of the most important reasons was TRADE. In the country you could grow your own food and make your own clothes, but if you could make a little more to sell you could buy extra luxuries. But to whom could you sell ? From whom could you buy ? The answer was travellers— *pedlars* [1] and merchants who came round ready to buy and

[1] You will find words printed like *this* in the Glossary on pages 88–90.

sell. So some of the first towns grew up because people built their houses at cross-roads or near a river bridge or ford. Then they sold food and lodging and goods to travellers and got richer. Others came because they heard there was money to be made—and so the town grew. By and by the townsfolk concentrated on making certain things like cloth or shoes and the country people began bringing in their food to sell and buying town goods in return. So the town became a market for the district where food and ' raw materials ' were exchanged for goods made by hand.

Some men made their towns close beneath the walls of the stone castles which the Normans built. Can you think why they chose to live there ? In some places towns grew round great monasteries. The monks needed workers— builders, blacksmiths, weavers, etc.—and the monastery had money to pay them, so the craftsmen settled outside the abbey gates and a town grew up there. Then some people settled near the sea where traders could find good harbours for their ships and could come in to buy or sell. Sometimes these ports were a long way up a river—as far up as ships could sail. London began like this. The first people there chose a good spot on some little hills by the river Thames, far enough up from the sea to be able to build a bridge, but not too far to stop the ships coming up. So the beginning of London was a small cluster of houses near London Bridge.

Lots of our towns just grew up of their own accord. But sometimes a great man—a lord or a bishop—decided to make a town. He chose a spot, perhaps drew a plan, and advertised for people to come and live in his new town. Salisbury was one of this kind : it was made by a great bishop.

People call Salisbury the 'sink' of Salisbury Plain. If you look at this map you will see why.

To begin with, there was nothing but a marsh with six rivers running into it. A short way up from the marsh, just where the hills began, there was a Norman castle with a ditch, a wall and a great earth *rampart* all round it. Close under the castle mound was a cathedral and a small town. This was called Sarisberie, or Old Sarum. Here is a plan showing the castle and town close together inside

4

the rampart. Notice the well. The first people to live here probably came because there was water to be had. They built the rampart, which is the oldest part.

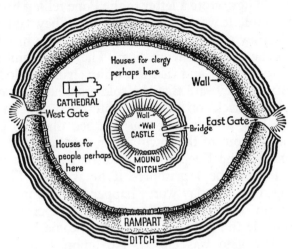

This is what the town probably looked like:

Some people must have found Old Sarum quite convenient, but after a time one group of people grew discontented. They were the clergy who belonged to the cathedral. They wrote a letter to the Pope telling him how uncomfortable it was living on this hill. They said it was so windy they could not hear themselves sing in Church and that they all got rheumatism. They complained that there were no trees and that the white chalk dazzled their eyes. Finally they said that the soldiers who guarded the castle played tricks on them and interfered with them.

If you look at the plan you will see that the priests could not get out of the town without going through one of the gates. The Keeper of the Castle had the keys and so could keep them prisoners if he wished. This was annoying, but one day worse happened. The priests had gone out in solemn procession to bless the crops in the fields outside the town and when they came back in the evening the gate was closed. No amount of shouting would persuade the soldiers to let them in. The priests were shut out for the night! This was the last straw, so they sent to the Pope begging permission to move the cathedral to a new town.

It was the Bishop of Salisbury, Richard Poore, who chose the site of the new town. Perhaps he stood on the hill at Old Sarum and looked at all the country spread around. Above him were the smooth rolling hills of the chalk downs. Below him were the water-meadows with the rivers winding through them. Where would you have put the new town? Bishop Poore chose a water-meadow called Myrfield. This lay low and was probably damp and not very good for the rheumatism the priests had complained about! But there were some good reasons for the choice. The rivers brought trade and from the

6

downs old grass tracks came down to meet just where the new town was to be placed. At any rate Bishop Poore said he had been guided in a dream and so Salisbury—or New Sarum—came to be where it is.

At Easter in the year 1219 a little temporary wooden chapel was built. In the summer the Bishop and the cathedral priests solemnly moved house from Old Sarum down to the water-meadow at Myrfield. What they moved into we can only imagine. Probably they lived in wooden huts, for to them the most important thing was to begin building the new cathedral. Workmen were gathered and set to work. It was very difficult to build a great cathedral on a bog. So, before they could lay foundations, they had to sink many *wattle hurdles* into the marsh to form a platform. At last, on April 28, 1220, they were ready to lay the foundation stones. There was a grand procession in which the Bishop and clergy wore their richest robes and country people from miles around flocked to see. Three stones were laid by Bishop Poore—one for Pope Honorius, one for the Archbishop of Canterbury, and one for himself. Then the Earl of Salisbury and his wife laid two, and four more were laid by the most important priests. You see, many people wanted to have a hand in building this new cathedral.

In those early days there was much to be done. What would you have got on with first : the cathedral or the houses ? Probably in Salisbury they built both side by side, for the cathedral certainly did not wait till last. The Bishop built himself a special house where he sat to plan his new town, for, like town-planners to-day, he did not wish his town to grow up all higgledy-piggledy. Soon workmen were making streets according to the Bishop's plan and people were beginning to ask if they could come

7

and live in the new town. All the time the builders and *masons* were at work and the white walls of the great cathedral were beginning to take shape.

This is how New Sarum was planned. Is it a good plan? Some things shown in this plan were built later.

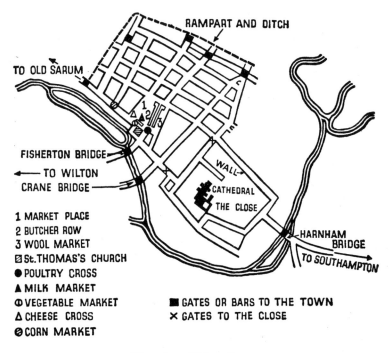

RAMPART AND DITCH

TO OLD SARUM

FISHERTON BRIDGE
← TO WILTON
CRANE BRIDGE

WALL

CATHEDRAL
THE CLOSE

HARNHAM
BRIDGE
TO SOUTHAMPTON

1 MARKET PLACE
2 BUTCHER ROW
3 WOOL MARKET
☒ St.THOMAS'S CHURCH
● POULTRY CROSS
▲ MILK MARKET
⊕ VEGETABLE MARKET
△ CHEESE CROSS
⊘ CORN MARKET

■ GATES OR BARS TO THE TOWN
✕ GATES TO THE CLOSE

The plan of New Sarum.

At first there were empty plots in the new town. Soon, however, these were filled as people came to live there. Bishop Poore made a bargain with the new townsfolk. Each man was to have a plot of land seven *perches* by

8

three perches in size. He was called a *burgess*. He was free to give, sell or let his plot to anyone else. He had to pay the Bishop a rent of 6d a year at Easter and Michaelmas. All this was written down in a piece of writing called a *charter*, so that there should be no mistake about it.

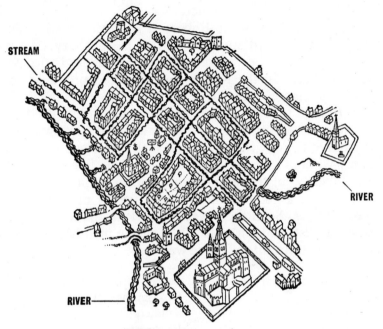

Salisbury 400 years later.

It was certainly better to be a burgess of Salisbury than a peasant in one of the nearby villages. When a peasant saw the burgess getting rich he often wished to live in the town too. But he could not do this freely for he was not allowed to leave his village without the permission of his lord-of-the-manor. If, however, he could slip away to

Salisbury (or another town) and stay there for a year and a day without being claimed, his lord could not fetch him back afterwards. Can you imagine an old burgess telling his grandchildren how he ran away and kept out of his lord's clutches until the year and day were up ? We know one of these stories because it was told in the King's law courts and written down there.

The story tells of one Robert of Alwardbury who ran away from his lord and later settled in Salisbury. Many years afterwards he was recognized and his lord tried to get him back. In the King's court the lord produced all Robert's relations who swore that he belonged to the lord. But Robert took no notice, saying that he had lived in Salisbury as a burgess for ten years and that 'such was the custom of the city that if anyone shall be for one year and a day without a claim on him, he shall be free for ever.' So Robert went free and the lord had to pay a fine.

To make a good town you need people of many different trades. Soon there were all sorts in the town. Here is an old list made in 1440 when all the men had to help re-dig the town ditch. There were :

Grocers and Drapers	Barber-surgeons and Cooks
Weavers	Goldsmiths and Blacksmiths
Fullers	Saddlers
Tailors	*Pewterers*
Brewers	*Vintners*
Shoemakers	Butchers and Tanners
Bakers	Dyers
Innkeepers	Painters

Bookbinders, *Parchment*-makers and Glovers
Carpenters, Bowmakers, *Tilers*, Builders and Arrow-makers.

Look up words you do not know in the Glossary.

By 1440 Salisbury was much larger than in the days of Bishop Poore and was full of prosperous burgesses whose riches came from trade. There were three reasons for their good trade.

The first was that Bishop Bingham, who was next after Bishop Poore, built a BRIDGE over the river Avon called Harnham Bridge. You can find it on the plan on page 8. Now all the foreign merchants who used to cross the river at Wilton a few miles away found it much more convenient to come to Salisbury. This was very good for Salisbury traders but very annoying to the men of Wilton. Here is a picture of Harnham Bridge to-day. There is a little chapel on it where prayers used to be said for the safety of travellers.

The second thing that made Salisbury rich was WOOL. All around on the chalk downs there were sheep who fed on the fine turf and produced some of the best wool in the south of England. Merchants of Salisbury used to ride out to the villages and buy the wool from the country people. They could sell it for good prices to the merchants from Flanders and Italy who wanted the best English wool to make into fine cloth. *Packhorses* carried the wool down to Southampton where it was shipped overseas.

The third thing that made the town rich was that in 1227 the King gave Salisbury a CHARTER in which he let them hold a market every week on Tuesday and a big fair once a year. It was easy for merchants to get to Salisbury from Southampton, as you can see from your map, and so the town attracted buyers and sellers who did good business together.

Here are two merchants riding into Salisbury.

CATHEDRAL BUILDERS

The most important thing in Salisbury was the Cathedral. In fact it was, as we have seen, the main reason why Salisbury was there at all. For many years the Bishop, the clergy and the people spent much effort and money on building the loveliest cathedral possible. They could put up their own houses quickly, but the cathedral must be built slowly and carefully to the glory of God.

First, the stone had to be quarried and hauled slowly to Salisbury in carts. For most of the cathedral they used stone from Chilmark, about 15 miles away. But they wanted to make the cathedral as beautiful as possible, and so, for the pillars, they fetched fine Purbeck marble all the way from Dorsetshire. This was the gift of Alice Brewere, a Dorset lady who promised to give marble for the cathedral for twelve years from her quarries in the Dorset hills. Find out, if you can, about how far they had to haul this. When it was ready it made pillars of a wonderful dark, polished grey-black. Everybody, rich and poor, wanted to give presents for the new cathedral. King Henry III gave oak-trees from his forest of Alderbury, and all over the country preachers collected money for it.

You can see on the next page a picture of men building the cathedral about 1230.

The workmen came from all over the country. They slept in wooden huts put up close by the cathedral. There were stone-cutters and masons, sculptors, carpenters, and labourers. They worked under the orders of a master mason and a master carpenter. For twenty years Robert the Mason was in charge of the actual building. He had a wooden hut, called the mason's lodge, where all the plans of the cathedral were spread out. The workmen had special rules about hours of work. In summer they began work at sunrise. When the bell rang they stopped for 20 minutes for breakfast. They had one hour off for dinner. Then they worked until the first bell sounded for Vespers, when they stopped to have a drink, but they had to start again when the third bell rang. Then they worked till sunset. In winter they worked as long as it was light. On all the feast days they had a holiday. Can you find out how long builders work to-day, and what rules their Trade Union makes for them?

The man who made all the plans for Salisbury Cathedral, the chief *architect*, was Elias of Dereham. He was not a practical builder at all, but I think he must have dreamt about cathedrals, for he helped to build several in England. While Salisbury was going up he was also directing building at Canterbury and Winchester cathedrals, and perhaps he did some building at Lincoln and Wells as well. Salisbury was all his own. I wonder whether he saw it all at once in a vision and then did the plans, or whether he thought it out a bit at a time? Unfortunately he died in 1245 before he could see it standing in front of him finished.

This is the plan of Elias of Dereham's cathedral:

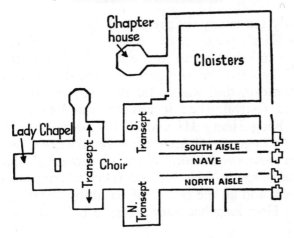

It is 450 feet long, and 203 feet wide in the principal *transept*. Compare these measurements with those of the biggest hall you know. Elias planned it all in the great style called the Early English style which belongs to the years between 1200 and 1300 (the thirteenth century). If you look carefully at the pictures on the next page, you will find out how to recognize this same style when you see it in other churches.

Slowly but surely the great walls began to rise according to Elias's plan. In five years the *Lady Chapel* was finished and they began to use it. Find this on the plan. Then they started on the transepts and the great *nave*. In 1258 the cathedral was so far finished, and there was a splendid festival when it was dedicated to the Virgin Mary. King Henry III and all his court came, and in front of a huge crowd Archbishop Boniface of Canterbury blessed the new cathedral. Can you picture all the court and the clergy in their brilliant robes of crimson, scarlet and gold, and all the people of Salisbury standing round about? How long had they taken to build the cathedral so far?

This was not the end of the building. Next they started on the *cloisters* and the *chapter-house*, where all the cathedral clergy held their meetings. And finally, a hundred years later, Robert Wyvill began to build the tremendous tower and spire. Do you know how high Salisbury spire is? It is 285 feet above the roof-ridge.

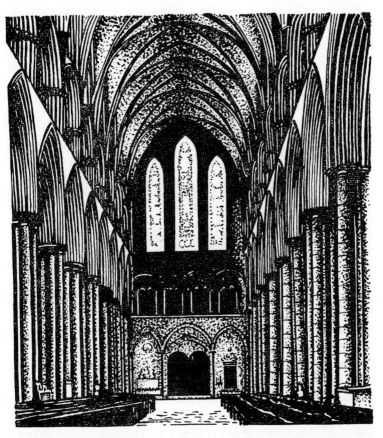

This spire was a dangerous thing to build, for, after all, Salisbury only stands on a marsh. Very soon people began to notice that the pillars were bulging because the spire was too heavy for them. They had to build two extra arches to keep the cathedral up, and even so, the tower and spire drove one of the supports into the ground. So for centuries the point of the spire has been 2 feet out of the straight. But the cathedral still stands, just as it was

finished about 1330. Do you think the spire looks crooked ?

The *canons* of the cathedral built their houses all round the *close* which surrounds the cathedral. Parts of those houses are still there to-day, and as you walk round you can picture all the different people who have lived in them. Besides the Bishop there were four chief men of the cathedral. The Dean was the head of the meeting (called the *chapter*) which the canons held in the chapter-house. The Precentor taught the choir-boys and looked after everything to do with the singing in the cathedral. The Chancellor kept a grammar school. The Treasurer looked after all the money. The canons attended the services in the cathedral, each one sitting in his own special stall (or seat), and they looked after the affairs of the cathedral. In the evenings they met in each other's houses for ' Potations ' (*i.e.* to drink together). A rule was made that Potations were to be held all together " in a place of sufficient size, with sufficient lights, round a fire, if it be possible, without smoke." I expect they had some merry times, but after a while these meetings were stopped.

An important part of their work was education. The Chancellor's grammar school was for the Salisbury boys and any others who came there. Then a college was built for students down by Harnham Bridge, and for some time there was a whole crowd of students coming to the cathedral for lectures. But the school which has lasted the longest is the *Choristers'* school, for it is still there in Salisbury to-day. I wonder if you would have liked to be a chorister. They lived all together in a house in the close with a Warden to look after them.

The choristers all wore blue gowns, with lambskin hoods when it was cold. They got a fresh outfit every year from their own tailor, and they also had their own barber and laundry woman. (Laundries lost things then as now, for once the laundry woman, Joan Flete, had to pay 15d for the choristers' shirts which she had lost.) Every day they had a singing practice with the Precentor (as well as ordinary lessons) and, of course, they had to sing in all the cathedral services. Woe betide the boy who sang out of tune, for the Precentor would probably whip him! But they found time for games in the close as well.

They did not always have a happy time. Once, for a time, no one looked after them at all, and they had to beg for bread. This is what Bishop Robert of Morteval wrote about them : " When like little children they asked for bread but could not find anyone to break a piece for them, they were compelled of necessity to go round to crave a beggar's dole each day from the houses of the canons, so as to get enough food to keep the wolf from the door." He was very angry about this, and made rules so that the choristers should always be properly looked after by a warden. Even then the boys were not always satisfied. One day they complained about the food and drink they got, so at the next chapter-meeting the Dean and canons had two loaves from the boys' table and a mug of their ale. Everyone tasted these, but I am afraid the boys were unlucky, for the chapter said : " This is good enough for choristers." I wonder if it was !

Many of the canons had other work to do, so they chose Vicars to take their place at the cathedral when they were absent. These vicars lived together in the Vicars' Hall, and there were very strict rules made for them. They must wear priests' gowns and not dress like other folk ; they must be inside the close before the *curfew* rang in the evening ; they must not eat meals outside the close or invite visitors inside. But they were not all good. Bishop Robert said they ran about the choir during service, leaping and skipping ! They sang flat, and egged the choir boys on to be naughty, and even brought their pet hounds into the cathedral. One of them, Adam Gore, swaggered round the town in a short, tight coat and a belt of marvellous size, and they liked to wear fringed hoods and hitch their priests' robes up short. They played ball in the close. They even played it in the cloisters, where they broke the library windows. One of them, William Warde, was punished for playing *knuckle-bones*, chess and dice in public places. He had to sit down among the lowest choristers in church.

One of the problems of the Dean and Chapter was how to keep the noise and trade of the town away from the close. The Bishop built a wall all round the close to keep the town out, and every night in winter, St. Anne's Gate and Harnham Gate were shut at 7 P.M. and the High Street Gate at 8 P.M. In summer these times were an hour later. No one was supposed to have a key, and the porter would not open the gate to anyone who was late. One old porter, Robert Dyer, who was on the job a long time, was very strict about this. Once, a vicar whom he had shut out, called him an old rattling churl. But I am afraid that a great many vicars got keys on the sly and came in and out as they pleased. Other people got in too. Sometimes travelling pedlars and fair men set up their stalls on the grass, or acrobats and men with wandering bears on a string would start to do tricks. It was difficult indeed to keep the close quiet, and people even fought and quarrelled inside the cathedral.

Perhaps the most exciting time in the year in Salisbury close was Christmastide. There were special services in the cathedral with elaborate and lovely music, and then there were feasts in all the houses. Above all, it was the choristers' festival, for on December 6, St. Nicholas's Day, they all elected a Boy Bishop. (St. Nicholas is the special saint of schoolboys; do you know the story about him?) The idea was that for a little while the order of things was turned upside down, so that children ruled and grown-ups obeyed. So, on the eve of the Holy Innocents' feast (December 28), the Boy Bishop was dressed like a real bishop, and went with all the choristers in solemn procession with burning tapers to the cathedral. There he took the Bishop's throne, all his fellows sat in the canons' seats, and the real canons had to sit down in the choristers' stalls. I expect this pleased the boys a lot! The Boy Bishop had his own special service, and sometimes he preached a sermon. After this the boys had a grand feast. We have a list of what was spent for one of these feasts (it was at York, not Salisbury, but it would probably be much about the same):

Bread 7d ; ale 21d ; veal and mutton 9½d ; sausages 4d ; 2 ducks 4d ; 12 chickens 2/6d ; 8 woodcocks and one plover 2/2d ; 3 doz. and 10 thrushes 19d ; small birds 3d ; wine 2/3d ; spices 11d ; 60 warden pears 5½d ; honey 2½d ; mustard 1d ; 2 lbs. candles 2½d ; flour 2d ; fuel 1½d ; to the cook 6d.

I must tell you about a sermon which a Boy Bishop once preached to his fellow choristers at Gloucester. This is what he said about them :

How boyishly they behave in church, how rashly they come into the choir without any reverence ; they never kneel to say any prayer but rudely squat down on their tails and jostle with their fellows for a place ; anon they start up out of the choir again, and in again and out again, and thus one after another to gad and gas abroad and so come in again, and cross the choir from one side to another and never rest nor serve God. (He points to one boy.) Look in his face and you would think that butter would not melt in his mouth, but, as smooth as he looks, I will not wish you to follow him if you know as much as I do ! Well, well, all is not gold that shines, nor all are innocents that bear the face of children !

Now, do you think he wrote that sermon himself, or did the old Precentor write it for him ?

ALL ROUND THE TOWN

Now we will find out what was going on in Salisbury five hundred years ago. Five hundred years ago takes us back to what we call the fifteenth century, between 1400 and 1500, when Salisbury had been growing for about 200 years. Finding out all we want to know is rather like a piece of detective work. We must use every possible clue and then add some imagination. But do not use imagination alone ! There are many clues about Salisbury and on page 81 you will find a list of all I have used.

Find out here about the Shops

Here are some of the market stalls :

The noise is terrific, for the market is full of people. Everyone selling the same thing has his stall in the same row, so the tradesmen shout against each other to attract customers. This is how one man described the scene :

Many a butcher, brewer, tailor and tinker,
Wool-weavers, linen-weavers, *toll-takers* in the market,
Cooks and their men were crying " Pies hot, all hot !
Good pork and good goose ! Come, come and dine ! "
Taverners told the same tale : " A drink of wine for nothing !
White wine, red wine, to wash the roast meat down ! "

You can see all sorts of people buying at the stalls. Here is a couple from the country who have come to buy pots for the house and cloth :

Look well at their clothes. This wife is actually buying cloth in the market instead of weaving it herself as her grandmother did. She has brought in home-grown produce to sell—eggs, butter, poultry, cheese—and with the money she buys town goods. Here are some country people coming into market with their loads :

One of the rules of the town is that no one may set up a shop or a stall just where he likes, but must find a place in the street or row set apart for the particular sort of goods he wants to sell. Strangers are given a special place and must pay a fee called *piccage* before they can drive stakes into the ground to set up their stalls. All the buying and selling is very neatly arranged. If you look again at the plan on page 8, you will see that there is one place for the wool-market, another for selling poultry and vegetables, and so forth. Many of the streets have names like Butcher Row, Cook Row, Smith's Row. Can you find the Cheese Cross on the plan? In 1416 the Town Council made a rule that country folk coming in with cheese, milk, grapes, plums, apples, pears, etc., should be compelled to keep to a place by the Cheese Cross. At the other end of the street is the Poultry Cross. Here the place seems alive with feathered birds and the country women who sit under the arches of the Cross cackle almost as loudly as the birds they sell. On the next page is a picture of the Poultry Cross to-day. Can you forget the twentieth-century things there and imagine what it was like in the fifteenth century?

If you look carefully you will see some houses which were probably there 500 years ago, like the Cross itself.

Some shops have stalls standing in front of them. Behind the stalls steps go up into the shop-keeper's workroom where you can see his men at work making goods to sell. This is very important because people like to see the things they buy being made. They think they are less likely to be cheated. Do you think this is a good idea? Some shops have no stall outside but an open window through which people can look. At night the stalls are taken down and the windows closed by wooden shutters. There are no huge plate-glass windows with grand displays of goods for sale. Can you think why not?

What shops would you like to visit? There is a stall with a bright red and orange roof over it which sells clay pots of all shapes and sizes. You can take your choice, for all the potters' stalls stand together in Pot Row. Or, if you want to be a little grander, you can go further down the street where all the pewterers live. They make plates, mugs, and jugs from a mixture of copper, tin and lead called English *pewter*. Here are some of the pewter things made in Salisbury :

The fishmongers' stalls are busiest on Fridays, when everyone eats fish. Here are some of the prices :

Best soles 3d doz. Best mackerel 1d each. Pickled herrings 2d a lb. Oysters 2d a gallon. Wriggling eels all fresh from a tub of water 25 for 2d.

Compare these prices with those of your nearest fish-monger to-day.

A 3

Not far off there is a very savoury smell which makes you feel hungry at once. This is where all the cook shops are ! You can see men running backwards and forwards from the great roaring fires, bringing out trays of steaming dishes to the stalls in the street. People stand round eating or buying dishes to take home. Here are some of the prices :

Best roast pig 8d	Best roast goose 7d
,, ,, hen 4d	,, ,, *capon* 6d
,, ,, partridge 3½d	,, ,, pheasant 13d
,, ,, rabbit 4d	Ten roast finches 1d
Five roast larks 1½d	Three roast thrushes 2d
Ten eggs 1d	

Take your choice !

A delicious smell of ginger, nutmeg and pepper comes from one row of shops. These are the spicers' or grocers' shops. Simon Corp, the spicer, has a dark, mysterious shop with shelves all round full of jars and bowls. He has a window with a flap shelf sticking out into the street on which he puts samples of spices in bowls. If you read the names on his jars you will find ginger, cinnamon, pepper, rice, raisins, almonds, *aniseed, saffron,* cloves, loaf sugar. The prices in this shop are high, for all these spices have to be brought across the sea from Venice and Genoa, and before that they travelled thousands of miles, partly across deserts. Still, many people buy spices, for they like their food well-flavoured. All the cooking recipes tell them to put in lots of spices. Remember you would not find in this spicer's shop several things that we get from our grocer's to-day. Tea and macaroni, for example, have only been brought to this country during the last 500 years.

There are three more shops we ought to see. One is a draper's. The district round Salisbury, as you know, is famous for wool, so the draper's shop has shelves stacked with fine soft cloth in many colours—deep blue, and bright scarlet, green and purple and rich brown. There are rolls, too, of rough, woollen *fustian* for the country folk who want hard-wearing clothes. One shelf has wonderful silks, velvets and brocades brought from Italy where they are very good at making rich materials. An important-looking lady is buying *ells* of violet silk and gold brocade. Her husband must be a rich merchant, for they are expensive. Here are some of the prices :

Velvet 20s ; cloth of gold £3 ; satin 6s 8d ; damask 9s ; linen 4s.

All these prices are for an ell of cloth. How much would a yard of each of these materials have cost ?

One draper's stall belongs to a woman. She is sitting there with a great pile of woollen rolls in front of her—red, green, azure blue, yellow, striped, checkered and scarlet. Listen to what a man is saying to her as he fingers a roll of mulberry red cloth :

Dame, what hold ye the ell of this cloth ?
Sir, ye can have it good cheap.
Yea truly. Take heed what I shall pay.
Four shillings for the ell, if it shall please you.
Here is no wisdom ! For so much would I have a good
     scarlet.
Sir, what is it worth ?
Dame, it is worth to me three shillings. Cut me a pair of
     gowns.

How much shall I cut ?

As much as sufficeth for a *surcoat*, a coat, a cloak and a pair of *hose*.

How bright this man will look when he has his cloth of mulberry red made up !

Next we must see a goldsmith's shop. This is a rich and splendid shop, with gold and silver dishes and wonderful jewellery. There is no stall outside here. The windows are barred and a watchman is on guard ! Inside there are chests all round and a counter in the middle. On the walls are splendid tapestries. The townsfolk like wearing jewellery —men as well as women—and they like it large. So here are great jewels to pin on your cap or shoulder, large rings and strings of beads—yellow amber, pink coral, black jet and so on. One lovely string is of silver beads and another of blue glass. If you want to see the most precious things you must ask the goldsmith to open the chest which has a special lock against burglars.

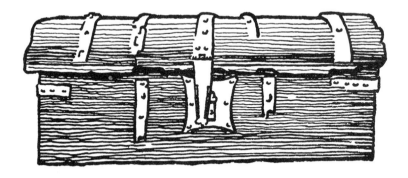

Do you know what *haberdashery* is ? To-day we have haberdashery departments in draper's shops ; in the fifteenth century they had separate haberdashers' shops.

You can get all kinds of things here.   This is a list of his
stock which one shop-keeper wrote. Compare the prices
with present-day ones.

2 doz. laces of red leather	8d	2 doz. coloured woollen	
1 doz. nightcaps	2s 3d	caps	16s
1 *russet* hat	6d	5 children's caps, red	
1 white hat	3d	and blue	2s 1d
4 prs of spurs	2s 9d	1 purse (sea-green colour)	6d
1 Cross painted	2s 4d	1 wooden gaming table	
1 set of jet beads	6d	with a set of men	6d
2 lb. of linen thread	2s	2 pairs of pen-cases with	
13 quires of paper	6s 8d	inkhorn	8d
1 wooden whistle	2d	4 eyeglasses	2d
1 gross of *points*	1s 6d	6 skins of parchment	6d

The eye-glasses are really a puzzle. Could they be
spectacles when four cost only 2d ? Do you know why
paper was so much more expensive in those days than
parchment ? To-day, it is the other way round.

We have not visited all the shops, for instance, the
butcher's, vintner's (or wine shop), tailor's, shoemaker's,
saddler's. But one shop we shall seek in vain is a chemist's
shop. Most medicines we get there to-day had not been
thought of in the fifteenth century. I don't know how you
would like the idea, but if you were ill then your father
would probably take you to a man called a barber-
surgeon. Yes—he really did do both jobs ! He was, I
fear, much too fond of his knife, and if he could not think
of anything else to do with his poor patients he opened a
vein for what is called blood-letting.

Have you noticed the kind of weights and measures
they use ? They sell things by the dozen or the gross,
by pounds and bushels, or by the ell. You should be

able to find out what all these mean. One of the great problems was to stop bad shop-keepers from cheating by using false weights and measures. Later on you will read how Salisbury people made rules to stop cheating and frauds.

Find out here about Clothes

To-day we wear whatever clothes we like. If a miner's wife saves enough money she has as much right to buy a fur coat as the prime minister's wife. So, on the whole, we all dress in very much the same way and it is not easy to tell just by looking at people how they earn their living. It was very different in Salisbury 500 years ago. Then everyone had a rank or place in society and had to dress according to that rank. Woe betide the person who tried to ' get above himself ' by dressing as if he belonged to a higher rank !

If you met a man or woman in the street in this dress you would know they were of noble rank.

They were allowed to spend a great deal on dress and both men and women liked to wear gowns of cloth of gold, velvet or silk, usually lined with another colour. A well-known man, Sir John Falstaff, whom you may have met in Shakespeare's plays, had two gowns of cloth of gold, one of velvet, one of blue satin lined with black silk and many cloth gowns and doublets lined or trimmed with fur. There were some wild fashions in head-dresses. Look at these !

As for shoes, they grew so long in the toes that men had to chain them up like this. They were so awkward for going upstairs that the owner usually stepped out of them and let his page carry them up.

 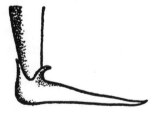 

The rich merchants of Salisbury, and especially their wives, liked to look like nobles. But the government wanted to keep people in their proper station, so laws were passed forbidding anyone under noble rank to wear cloth of gold or expensive furs like *sable* or *miniver*. These laws were not always kept ! A man named Hoccleve complained that you could not tell nobles in the street because knaves copied their lords. Do you think it really mattered if they did ?

If you met a rich merchant of the fifteenth century out with his wife they would have looked rather like the couple in this drawing.

This picture is from an engraving in brass in a church. These merchants liked to feel that their names would be remembered after they were dead, so memorial brasses like this were often put in the church where they were buried. There are many of these brasses in the southern part of England, so when you visit an old church remember to look for them. They are often covered by the floor-matting.

You would easily recognize craftsmen and labourers in the street, for they would be wearing short tunics, hose and perhaps a hat, like the man on the next page. They looked very sober, for no one with an income of less than £40 was allowed to wear gold, or decorated girdles, or *kerchiefs* costing more than 3s 4d, and no labourer could buy cloth costing more than 2s a yard or hose at more than 1s 3d the pair. These laws about what clothes people might and might not have were called *sumptuary laws*. Why do you think they were passed? Do you think such laws were good? Try to think of a reason for your answer.

Here you will find out about
Streets, Gates and Walls

Have you ever visited a town where there were old houses in which each of the upper storeys stuck out a little beyond the one below, closing in over narrow streets? Salisbury streets in the fifteenth century were like this—narrow, dirty and smelly.

The real reason why the streets were so dirty was that there were no dustmen to collect rubbish and no proper drains. Going down the street you had to step over all sorts of rubbish, and also keep out of the way of things thrown out of the windows. Salisbury people tried to stop this, but I am afraid some people would not keep rules. The butchers especially had to be watched. They threw all their remains in the river ! And the pudding wives, or women who used to make sausages and black puddings, used to do the same. At last the Town Council made a rule that they could only throw away their refuse in a part of the river not near the main street. Anyone who broke this rule paid a fine of 5 shillings.

One very useful thing about the rivers of Salisbury was that the people could get plenty of water in the town. They cut channels down the middle of the main streets and had running water flowing through. You may think this was awkward for traffic, but remember, there were no motors or buses, only heavy carts, horses and people on foot. On the next page is a picture of the street in which they sold vegetables. You will see the stream

35

running down the street. Look at the plan on page 9, where wavy black lines show the streams running through the town.

36

Of course on a dark night people sometimes fell into the streams, which was a nuisance for them; but it was very useful to have running water at your door. Remember there was no town supply laid on. When you wanted water you did not turn the tap but went out into the street and dipped it out of the stream. This was handy but it was also very dangerous. Just think of all the rubbish which went into those streams, and then imagine drinking that water! Are you surprised that sometimes a terrible epidemic of some disease swept through the town?

The people of Salisbury did not bother much about providing town water or street lighting or town drains, but they did bother about town defences. Most towns at this time tried to guard themselves against outsiders by building some sort of defences. You can easily think out the reasons for yourself. Most of the towns built walls. This is what a walled town looked like:

Do you know any towns with walls or gates (or parts of them) left standing to-day ?

Salisbury burgesses did not build a wall round their town. Actually they got permission from the king to put up a stone wall with towers, but for some reason they never did it. I wonder why not. But they needed some protection, for there were robbers in the lonely parts of Salisbury Plain. So in 1308 the Mayor got permission to dig a ditch all round the town " on account of the entering of robbers which we feared." It took them a long time to make, but in the end they had a broad dry ditch, with perhaps a *palisade* on top, running right round the part of the town not protected by the river. Look at the plan again and see where it ran. At first they had bars or chains put across the main roads out of the town by night, so that no one could steal in or out. Then later they built two good gates at the end of Castle Street and Winchester Street.

Although the town did not build a wall, the Bishop did. I think he was not quite sure what would happen if the townsfolk got angry one day and mobbed the cathedral clergy. And they certainly did quarrel sometimes ! So, as we have seen, he built a stone wall round the cathedral, enclosing with it the space round and all the houses in which the clergy lived. So this was called the Close. The Bishop's great problem was to get stone for this wall without paying a lot to cart it from quarries some distance away. The Bishop had a bright idea. Just a mile away, up in Old Sarum, there were heaps of stone in the old cathedral which was slowly falling down. So he sent up carts to bring down loads to build the walls. They even used some of the carved bits of stone, and to-day, as you walk along by the wall in Salisbury, you can see these

38

carved pieces sticking out. Here is one of the gates on the road from the close into the town :

To-day you can come in and out of Salisbury without anyone taking the slightest notice, but in those days there would be a real to-do when you arrived outside the town gate. If you were a merchant you would have to show all your goods and probably pay money (called toll) on them, whilst the watchman might question you carefully about your business, for they did not want any suspicious characters to get in. Things were usually lively at the town gate, and when the townsfolk had nothing better to do, they went down to one of the main gates to watch strangers coming in and gossip about them. On the next page is the scene at a town gate as it was drawn by someone living about 1400.

The burgesses were not very friendly to strangers. They wanted to keep all their advantages for themselves, and they were always afraid that strangers would make a profit out of them, or get the better of them in some way. Everyone who was not a burgess of Salisbury was an outsider or ' foreigner '; you needed him to trade with, but you had to keep him in his place! Do you think that heaving a brick at his head is a good way of putting a foreigner in his place? One day there was a quarrel at the town gates; one of the burgesses called a stranger " a false knave and a roughfooted Scot " and threw a weight at his head. The Town Council certainly did not think this was the way to treat foreigners, and the burgess was heavily fined.

Here you will find out about Houses

I expect you have already decided that some of these Salisbury burgesses must be getting rich on their trade. What would you have spent your money on if you had been in their place? Of course they had their own ideas, and one of these was to build themselves fine houses. There was a lot of building going on in Salisbury between 1400 and 1500. Most of the houses had a timber frame with walls made of a lattice-work of thin wood covered thickly with plaster. Many of these houses are still standing to-day, and in some places you can see just what the lattice and plaster work looks like. Here is one of them:

On the next page you will see some builders starting on a house of this kind.

This is the house which John A'Port built for himself in 1425. The ground floor has been made into a shop nowadays.

Now we will visit the house of Richard Gilbert. It is four storeys high and looks very fine outside, for the black timbers are carved in patterns, and there are wooden figures and faces carved on the doorposts and at the beam-ends. These are painted with gold and scarlet. The windows have glass in the top half, but only wooden shutters below. Richard is very proud of that glass, because it is quite a new thing in England and therefore very expensive. At the bottom of the house there is a big stone cellar with the steps down from the street. This is his warehouse, where he keeps all his stock. On the ground floor is his shop, and then you go up a narrow wooden stair to the first floor, where you come into the chief room of the house called the hall. It is very pleasant and cheerful, for the walls have rich red-brown tapestry showing exciting pictures of men hawking and hunting, all in green, red and blue. There is a roaring fire on a big open hearth with a wide chimney, and a carved stone mantelpiece, painted blue and red. In the middle is the long trestle table where Richard and all his family and his workmen take their meals.

Richard and his wife have two handsome carved chairs like this at the head of the table. The others sit on benches and stools. There is a fine chest which is used for storing things and also to sit on. It has animals and birds carved on it and is painted in red and gold. A big carved cup-board has pewter and silver plates and cups on its shelves. On the walls there are twisted iron holders for torches and candles. When they light flaming torches all round the hall it looks grand.

At one end is a carved wooden screen painted in blue, red and gold. From behind this come all the good smells from the kitchen, the larder, the bakehouse and the brewhouse. Richard has a *buttery* full of loaves, beef, and barrels of beer.

Then we go up a little winding stair to the next floor, where there is a comfortable parlour in which Richard and his wife sit in the evenings. Next to it are two bedrooms—the great chamber in which Richard and his wife sleep, and the little chamber for their children. The parlour has a pattern in scarlet and white painted on the walls and some carved wooden furniture, a table, a chest and some stools. Here is Richard sitting comfortably by his fire :

In the great chamber Richard has a large and comfortable bed of which he is very proud. Many people still sleep on straw but he has bought a bed with four posts and blue curtains hung all round ; on it he has a mattress, feather bed, sheets, blankets and a green coverlet. There are two chests here: one is a large one with all their clothes in it and also the steel cap and leather jacket that Richard puts on when he has to fight for the town; the other is a small one containing all Richard's money. Why do you think he keeps it up here? Where would he keep it to-day?

Up above, again, in the attics, sleep Richard's apprentices and two of his servants. They have no fine beds—only straw mattresses on the floor!

Richard is a fairly rich man and when he can, he likes to buy the kind of things that nobles have. Richard is very fond of one or two of his valuables. He has a large silver bowl (called a *mazer*) with a lid finely patterned, and a silver salt-cellar, and he actually has 141 silver spoons. It is in the fashion already to have spoons for meals, but most folk do not own so many.

One of the best houses in Salisbury has just been built by John Halle. They say he owns all the sheep on Salisbury Plain, and he certainly behaves like a lord. He would be pleased if he knew that his house was going to last longer than many other houses in Salisbury. For if we jump forward to our own century again for a moment, John Halle's house is still there. But I think you will be surprised to find, if you visit it, that you are walking into a cinema! No—John Halle did NOT build the cinema; that is very new, but part of John Halle's house has been kept as the entrance hall of the cinema. Notice the fine carved woodwork in the picture on the next page.

Inside, we find ourselves in the banqueting hall. It has a minstrels' gallery, a carved timber roof and brilliant stained-glass windows with coats of arms of some of the noblest families in the land in them. This tells us that

John Halle's house at Salisbury.

John Halle, the wool merchant, was the friend of great lords, but he did not forget where his money came from. So, beside the proud coats of arms, he put his merchant's mark, the sign that he was a Merchant of the Staplers.

Some people like to paint stories on their walls—of King Arthur or Abraham and Isaac or other Bible stories. You can still see one of these in a Salisbury house to-day.

Here is a picture of the Great Inn of the George:

This inn was certainly standing in the High Street of Salisbury in the fifteenth century, and it is still standing there to-day.

If we go back again and visit the George in the fifteenth century, we shall find it full of hurry and bustle, with travellers riding up and stable boys holding prancing horses or bringing them from the stables behind. This

47

is the most famous inn in Salisbury. Perhaps it began as a pilgrim hostel but now in the fifteenth century it houses noblemen and merchants as they travel through Salisbury. It belongs to the Mayor and Town Council, and from the town accounts we find out that they have let it to John Grymes, a saddler, for the rent of £12 13s 4d a year. There are twelve rooms in it for guests. The most important rooms are the Principal Chamber, the Earl's Chamber, the Oxford Chamber, the Middle Chamber, the Squire's Chamber, the Lombard's Chamber. You can imagine for yourself the kind of people who might sleep in some of these rooms. The Lombards would be rich merchants from Italy. (Do you know a street in London where they used to stay?) This is a picture of one of the top rooms in the George:

Look at the roof-tree which holds up the roof. THAT was there 500 years ago.

I wonder if you would have liked to sleep in this room 500 years ago. This is all the furniture it contained: three beds containing fifteen planks, one old table of beech for meals, one bench of elm, one bench of oak, one cupboard. The list does not say anything about mattresses or bedclothes, so they probably slept on the bare boards! Start by copying the picture opposite and then draw the rest of the room as you think it looked in the fifteenth century.

Some of the stable-boys at the George in the fifteenth century have seen exciting times. Once there was a big fire in which people escaped by the skin of their teeth. In 1449 at 8 o'clock one evening there was a fierce fight between the armed men of Lord Moleyns, who was staying in the George, and the townsmen of Salisbury. Why Salisbury folk were angry with him we do not quite know, but it was all to do with a man named Jack Cade who led a rebellion against the King.

Some Salisbury folk do not have very grand houses. We will visit John the Cook-upon-the-Ditch now. As you can tell from his name, he lives down by the town ditch. He has no glass in his windows, for he cannot afford it, but he has stretched oiled linen tight across his windows and this lets in quite a lot of light. Inside, he has a hall, like Simon, over his shop, but not a very big one. He cannot afford tapestry on the walls, so he has painted patterns all over them. The floor is covered with rushes and he has a large trestle table. Because he is a cheerful man he has painted a border of roses all round it. He and his wife have an armchair each, and besides this they have four stools, a long bench and a little one by

49

the wall covered with red and green cloth. There is a kitchen behind the hall, and from this you climb up a ladder into the one bedchamber in the house. Here John and his wife have a rough bed with a straw mattress and blankets on it, and all the rest of the family sleep on the floor.

People in Salisbury are very fond of gardens. Some burgesses have made theirs most pleasant. These gardens are behind the shops. Sometimes there is a passage-way straight through from the street with a bright patch of flowers framed in the archway at the end. If you walk through you will find a square garden enclosed by walls and laid out with neat paths and beds in a pattern. Sometimes there is a little private arbour cut out of thick privet or yew with a bench to sit on. Here are two ladies in a garden :

This is a list of some of the plants they grow :

To eat : onions, leeks, peas, cabbage, lettuce, nettles, sage, thyme, saffron, rosemary, roses, violets, apples and pears.

Flowers : poppies, geraniums, daffodils, lilies of the valley.

I am sure you will be surprised at some of the things they eat ! Notice that they have no potatoes. When did these first come to England ? You would often find Salisbury folk sitting in their gardens, the burgess perhaps on the bench in his arbour drinking wine and the ladies making garlands for themselves, or even playing ball !

One of the things I am sure you would notice in fifteenth-century Salisbury is that none of the houses has a number. Some of the bigger ones, however, have signs hung out. As you go along the streets these are some of the signs you see : Swan, Beaver, Ram, Gander, Sprat, Cock, Lion. Some men get called after the sign of their house. So you might meet Walter atte Goat, John atte Bell, Thomas atte Red Dore, Simon Sprat and so on. This is one way in which surnames began. Can you think of some more surnames which might in the beginning have been house signs ?

Here you will find out about Food

The burgesses of Salisbury eat two good meals a day : dinner at 12 noon and supper at 5 P.M. Most people only have bread and beer for breakfast, so by dinner they are really hungry. Everyone sits down together in the hall— the master and his family at the top of the long trestle table, then the workmen and servants in order of import- ance, and down at the bottom the noisy young apprentices.

Most people now have linen tablecloths, and in the middle of the table, marking off the part where the master's family sits from the lower part, there is a large silver salt-cellar, often in the shape of a ship.

For plates some use wooden platters and some still cut a thick slice of bread (called a trencher) for each person. On this you put your food and at the end you can either eat your plate or throw it to the dogs. A nice easy way of avoiding the washing-up ! Each person brings his own knife, and many now have spoons as well ; a few have forks, but most people still use their fingers. When everyone is sitting down, the meal is carried in from the kitchen, still on the roasting spit. First, the master cuts off a piece for himself, and then the joint goes down the table, each one cutting off what he wants. They eat a lot of meat. Here is the menu for quite an ordinary meal :

Brawn, bacon, beef, boiled chicken, roast goose, pork, veal, lamb ;
Spiced apples, pears, bread and cheese, spiced cakes.

To drink there is ale and *mead* (made from spices and honey) in pewter mugs. People certainly do eat a lot of good food. Here is another menu:

First Course :   soup, bacon, pork, tripe, roasted ox-tongue.
Second Course : salt beef, mutton, ham.
Third Course :   fine fat cheese, tarts, apples.

On Fridays and in Lent everyone eats fish. They like herrings and mackerel, salmon and halibut. Eels are very popular and oysters too. They are very fond of elaborate pastries. The outside pastry cases (called coffins) are made in all kinds of shapes and then filled in different ways. Here is some fifteenth-century advice on how to eat them :

> All those pies that be good and hot,
> Open them at the top of their coffin cot,
> All that be cold and stiff within their crust,
> Always at the middle open them you must.

Try this method on a pork pie !

Poor people do not get nearly so much variety or quantity in what they eat. Many have beans and bacon until they are heartily tired of them. Herrings and other fish, eggs and cheese make a change, but they seldom get meat except on a very great feast day.

HOW PEOPLE WORKED

To-day most workers belong to a Trade Union. If you know a Trade Union member, find out what his union is and what it does. In Salisbury in the fifteenth century all the craftsmen belonged to Guilds. There are a good many differences between a Trade Union and a Guild. The most important is that Trade Union members are all employees (men employed by someone else). In the fifteenth century everyone in a certain trade belonged to the same guild. These were masters who owned the businesses, men who worked for them (called journeymen) and apprentices learning the trade. They banded themselves into guilds for various reasons : to help each other, to improve and protect the craft and to enjoy jolly times together. Another reason for guilds was that people were afraid of cheats. They were afraid that masters might cheat workmen, and workmen masters, and both the customers. So the town government decreed that anyone who wanted to set up in any trade must join the guild and obey its rules. No outsiders were allowed.

Turn back to the list of trades on page 10. This is really a list of the Craft Guilds in Salisbury in 1440. A meeting was called of the heads of all the guilds to arrange about sharing out the work when the town ditch was being re-dug and this is the list of the guilds that sent representatives.

Before you were allowed to practise a trade you had to learn it properly by being apprenticed to a master for several years. Then you worked as a journeyman until you had saved up enough money to pay your entrance fees as a master and buy a workshop. But before you were allowed to set up as a master, the officials of your guild examined your work and record to ensure that you would not let the guild down. As a matter of fact, by 1440 the masters were beginning to make the entrance fees so high that many journeymen could never save up enough and so they remained employees all their lives. Still, there was always the chance for an industrious journeyman to become a master.

Rules of work were very strict in the guilds. No one could begin his work before sunrise or continue it in the dark after the curfew bell had sounded. Can you see the reason for that rule ? No one could work after dinner on Saturday, or Sunday, or on the Church festival days. Every guildsman had to help his brother craftsman in any way he could—even help him finish a piece of work which had to be done in a hurry. No one was allowed to sell his goods at a price below the fixed one, or to try and undercut his brother guildsman in any way. And no one was allowed to start selling till a fixed hour in the morning (generally 9 or 10 o'clock). Can you see the point of this ?

If a master quarrelled with his apprentices or journeymen, a ' love-day ' was arranged when the guild officials tried to settle the quarrel.

One of the things the guilds cared most about was looking after the guild brethren when they were sick or old or in trouble. They all had special rules about this. Here is one of them :

> If it so befall that any of the brotherhood fall into poverty through old age, that he may not help himself, or through any other chance, through fire or water, thieves or sickness, or any other hap, so it be not through his own fault, then he shall have in the week 14d from the common box.

Each of the guildsmen paid a yearly contribution into a common box, and besides helping brethren in distress this money was used to pay for the funerals of poor brethren, to keep lighted candles on the special altar of the guild and to pay for prayers for the souls of dead guildsmen.

As you know, a great many people in Salisbury got their living by wool. Up on the chalk downs there were thousands of sheep, and each year after sheep-shearing great bales of wool were woven into cloth by many workers in the city. Women and children did the spinning, and you could hear a spinning wheel humming in nearly every house as you passed by. The yarn went to members of the Weavers Guild for weaving into cloth. This was the oldest guild in the city and some of its members did a roaring trade. We can find out from the town accounts that Salisbury produced 6,600 rolls of cloth in one year.

From the weavers the cloth went to the dyers to be dyed and then to the fullers who ' fulled ' or finished it. You would be surprised at the way they did this, for they put the cloth in running water and then beat it with

55

hammers. All the fullers had their houses down by the streams where they set up their mills and racks. Finally the cloth was stretched out to dry on frames called *tenters* in special open spaces called *tenter-grounds*.

I wonder if you could guess how many people were employed making cloth in Salisbury at this time. We have a clue because in 1420 the town government held a meeting of all the cloth-workers to try and improve the quality of the cloth made. These are the people who came to the meeting :

> 81 master weavers, 207 journeymen weavers, 4 stewards of the Weavers' Guild, 61 master fullers, 31 journeymen fullers, 2 stewards of the Fullers' Guild.

The town officials were very particular about the quality of the cloth produced. There was a special law, called the Assize of Cloth, which said exactly how wide it should be, and before any piece could be sold, an official of the town, called the *Aulnager*, had to come round and inspect it. He measured it and opened out the whole roll, looking for bad patches. You see, one of the tricks bad weavers tried to play was to weave good cloth at the beginning and end of the roll and use bad wool in the middle. When the Aulnager had made sure that the whole roll was all right, he sealed it with his special seal. The cloth had to be sold where the town government said it should be. If you tried to give them the slip you were fined £20. Selling to foreigners was strictly forbidden unless you got a licence from the Mayor. Actually, a good many merchants did get licences, for large waggon-loads of cloth used to go down to Southampton for export to Flanders or Italy. Of course people tried to play tricks. John Corscombe made a counterfeit (or false) seal with which he sealed his own cloth, but he was caught with twenty-one striped cloths all falsely sealed, and accused before the King's Justices. One of the ways they tried to stop this kind of thing was by making every weaver have a special mark on his cloth, so that the Aulnager could tell at once who had woven any piece of cloth.

You can easily picture to yourselves many of the other jobs to be done at that time. Bakers, butchers, and brewers need no explanations. Potters and pewterers are important. Here are some of them at work :

Pewterers had to work by special rules in order to keep up the quality of English pewter. When they made flat dishes they must use 26 lb. of copper to a hundredweight of tin. For pots and candlesticks they were allowed the same amount of lead and tin. They had searchers who came round to see that they didn't make cheap stuff.

Tanning and leather work were also extremely important. Think of all the things you can do with leather ! Tanners' work was messy but very skilled. The skins (or hides) came to them straight from the butchers and had first to be scraped, soaked and rubbed with lime in order to get rid of all the flesh and hair. Then they were put into the great *vats* full of tan. The tan was made out of oak bark, and there were stern rules against using any other bark. In these tanning vats some of the hides were left for a long time, even as much as a year. Then they came out as lovely soft leather which could be dyed all sorts of colours—purple, scarlet, brown, etc. The tanners lived down by the streams for they used the running water, and the town officials tried to keep them outside the town, if possible, because tanning made dreadful smells and fouled the water. When the leather

had been tanned it was used by saddlers, shoemakers, and men of other trades. In this picture are some shoemakers at work.

In Salisbury the Shoemakers Guild was important. It had a hall of its own for meetings. We do not know where this was in the fifteenth century, but later on it was in the house which is shown on page 41.

58

HOW PEOPLE PLAYED

Members of the guilds liked to play as well as work together. So nearly every guild had its special feast days when they all went to church and then had a grand feast. Many guilds wrote down in a book all the rules about how these festivals were to be kept, and we still have some of these records. In Salisbury, for instance, you can still see the book of the Tailors Guild. Here is part of a page from it :

From this book we can find out everything the Tailors used to do at their great feast on St. John the Baptist's Day at midsummer. First of all, some days before, the stewards of the guild went round to warn all the brethren and sisters to have their special dress (or *livery*) ready and the proper number of wax tapers and torches. Then they were all bidden to come to a feast for three nights before midsummer; on the first night a man and his wife paid 8d, on the second night 4d, and on the third 6d. The book does not say what they feasted on, but on another occasion they had pieces of beef, sides of mutton, and boiled chicken. Then on Midsummer Eve there was a grand pageant when the whole town turned out to set the Midsummer Watch. The Mayor and Council rode in a procession all round the town and all the guilds with them. But the Tailors had the best place, for they rode at the head and they carried in front of them the huge figure of a giant. Beside him went two gentlemen, one carrying a great two-handled sword, and the other a mace. There was also a little page on a hobby-horse called Hobnob, and *morris dancers* in quaint dresses with little bells hung on them. You can still see the Tailors' giant in the Salisbury Museum. Here he is with Hobnob:

But I don't think these are the same figures that they used in the fifteenth century. You see, the giant was stuffed full of paper and rags and the rats and mice found him very good to eat ! Sometimes they put arsenic inside him to keep the rats away !

When the procession was over, the stewards of the Tailors Guild went to St. Thomas's church and decorated the chapel of the Blessed Virgin Mary and St. John, which is inside it, with red roses and lit a wax taper in front of the altar. By 8 o'clock next morning the stewards were marching all round the town with a minstrel calling all the guild brethren to come in procession at 9 o'clock carrying their lights to St. John's chapel. The Mayor and Council came too, and there special prayers were said. These were written in a special part of the old Tailors' book which was called the Bede-Roll. This is how it begins :

> Ye shall pray for the tranquillity and peace of all Christian realms and in special for this realm of England. Also ye shall pray for the good state and prosperity of the King and Queen and the prince and for their progenitors. Also ye shall pray for the souls of all the brethren and sisters, being quick and dead, and in special for the souls of those which were special good doers in their lives. Also ye shall pray for the souls that are departed out of this world.

Then there is a list of all the guild members who left money or land or possessions to the guild when they died. Some were very rich, but some left quite humble gifts, like Harry Hyll who left one brass pot.

After the service, they all went to the guildhall for the crowning feast of all. Every master of the craft paid 12d for this dinner for himself and his wife, or 8d if he was alone, and a woman paid 6d. Journeymen paid 4d, and sat together at one table. Finally, after the feast, they all marched down to the little chapel of St. John on Harnham Bridge where the journeymen lit their own special light, and then back to the hall where they ended the festivities with "a drinking in the most godly wise." Who knows how much they ate and drank in those days and what they felt like at the end of it ! The book does not give the menu for the great feast but it might have been something like this :

First Course :   Pottage, baked duck, capons roasted in syrup, roast veal, roast pig, herons.
Second Course : Roasted rabbits, pheasant, *venison*, hedge-hogs.
Third Course :   Cokyntryce, a peacock roasted and served in feathers, a pastry castle with silver flags, filled with sweets, pears and peaches in syrup.

The recipe for cokyntryce will amuse you. Here it is :

Take a capon, scald it, clean it and smite it in two at the waist. Do the same to a pig. Then sew the fore-part of the capon to the hind-part of the pig, and the hind-part of the capon to the fore-part of the pig. Stuff them and roast.

Well, all good things come to an end, and the Tailors had to go back to work. But they were so determined to keep their feast going that they wrote : " This feast shall be yearly kept while the world standeth." The world still stands but the Tailors' feast in Salisbury has gone !

Many other guilds had feasts and processions too. The Mayor and Council had a guild of their own called the

Guild of St. George. **On St** George's Day they rode in solemn procession carrying a figure of St. George in armour to St. Thomas's church. It must have been a fine sight, for the Mayor and Council were dressed in crimson and scarlet gowns, and behind came all the guilds in their liveries, the minstrels and the morris dancers. After they had prayed in church for the city and its departed citizens, a play was acted in which St. George killed the dragon and then the Guild of St. George had a great feast.

There was another gorgeous pageant on St. Osmund's eve (July 15), for he had been a great bishop of Old Sarum. On Corpus Christi Day all the guilds processed again and acted plays. At one Corpus Christi feast one guild consumed 10 lambs, 2 calves, 16 pigs, 70 chickens and 100 pigeons !

Do you notice that these guildsmen go to church first, before they make merry ? You see, the guilds held their festivals on saints' days, often the day belonging to their own patron saint. So their holidays were really religious holidays on which they first met in church to give glory to God and then went to their guildhall for feasting and fun. Each guild had its own altar in one of the churches, and there you would often find candles burning in memory of guild members who had died.

One rich merchant, William Swayne, spent a lot of money on building a beautiful guild chapel for the Tailors in the south aisle of St. Thomas's church. You can still see this to-day.

The windows were filled with richly coloured glass, the roof carved and brightly painted, the walls covered with Biblical pictures. In various places he put his own coat of arms and merchant's mark, whilst carved in the roof are the words : " Pray for the soul of William Swayne and Chrystian his wife." Merchants and craftsmen who made money liked to spend it for the salvation of their souls and on making their churches beautiful. If you look carefully at the old churches you visit you will often discover that someone of this kind has built a side aisle or a chapel. Often he left his own special mark somewhere in it. (I know a church window with a pair of scissors carved on it to show it was put there by a clothier.) Do people who get rich use their money in this way to-day ?

In Salisbury many citizens gave money in the fifteenth century to repair and enlarge St. Thomas's church. They made it much bigger than the little old church which had been built when the town was small and new. They gave it large windows to let in more light, wide side-aisles and a beautiful carved roof. On some of the pillars they carved the names of the citizens who gave them. Over the chancel archway they painted a tremendous Doom Painting of the Last Judgement, which showed the righteous souls rising from their tombs to go to heaven and the unrighteous being cast down into hell. When the people of Salisbury sat in front of this picture it gave them solemn thoughts and perhaps it scared the evil-doers.

The style in which these Salisbury citizens rebuilt St. Thomas's church is called the Perpendicular style. Find out if any of the churches round you are built in this style. If so, you will find that they were built or altered about the same time as St. Thomas's.

Perhaps you are thinking that going to church and then having a feast is, after all, not such a very exciting form of amusement. But there was plenty of fun and games in Salisbury, in the evenings, on Sundays and on feast-days.

In the next set of pictures you can study for yourself how people amused themselves 500 years ago. Can you give a name to each picture?

On Shrove Tuesday all the apprentices of the town had a fine game of football. They kicked the ball through all the streets, but I am afraid the rules were not very good, for the game often ended in a fight!

HOW SALISBURY WAS GOVERNED

The most important question to ask about any town is : How is it governed ? Do the townsfolk manage their own affairs or does someone from outside rule them ? At first the Bishop ruled Salisbury, for he had built it, but soon he decided to give the people some part in managing their own town. He allowed them to have a Mayor and town government of their own. Then they felt much more independent, for only the most important towns had their own Mayors.

The first Mayor on the list is Reginald de Wych in 1261, but there may have been one or two before him. To govern the town they chose twenty-four men called aldermen and forty-eight others to assist them. All these met together, probably in St. Thomas's church, and elected their Mayor out of the twenty-four. The Mayor, the twenty-four and the forty-eight made the town government. Because Salisbury was still under its Bishop, the Council had to go and ask his approval of the Mayor they had chosen. The new Mayor promised to obey him, but his real promises were made to the city of Salisbury. He probably took an oath which went something like this :

I will keep the city of Salisbury with all my mind and power, no man by reason of kin or friendship sparing, no man by reason of hatred grieving. I will be faithful to the community and will keep secret its counsel.

What does your Town Council do ? Could you make a list of some of the matters it has to attend to ? Here is a rough list of all the things the Mayor and Council of Salisbury had to look after in the fifteenth century :

Defence of the Town.	Searching out Fraud.
Watch and Ward.	Sending M.Ps. to Parliament.
The Streets.	Town Festivals.
Fire.	

In the fifteenth century there were many bands of armed men about and a good deal of fighting, so the first duty of the town government was the defence of the city. Many towns guarded themselves with walls, but, as we have seen, Salisbury never did this, but only dug a wide ditch with a rampart. This took a long time to do and all the different guilds had to take part in the work and provide money for the job. The main roads and bridges that led into Salisbury were guarded either by chains or by gates. Look again at the plan on page 8 and see where these defences were. It was very important to have armed men ready to defend these gates and ditches if brigands were seen riding up. So every burgess of Salisbury had to be ready to fight for his town when the alarm was given.

Twice a year everyone was summoned to a ' muster of arms.' This meant that they all had to come fully armed for inspection. Poor burgesses each had to have a knife, dagger, or hatchet, and richer ones a coat of mail, shield, bow and arrows, and sword. To give the alarm they probably had a great bell. This is the rule that another town, Hereford, made about this same time, and perhaps Salisbury had the same.

Concerning our bell, we will have it in a public place where our chief bailiff may come as well by day as by night, to give warning to all men living within the city. And we do not say it ought to ring unless it be for some terrible fire burning, or for any common contention whereby the city might be

67

terribly moved, or for any enemies drawing near unto the city or if the city is besieged. All manner of men of what degree soever ought to come at any such ringing with their weapons.

I wonder if anyone ever rang the bell for a joke, and, if so, what happened to him?

Sometimes the burgesses got a command from the King to send some men to fight in his wars. They did not like this at all, for it cost them much money and took them away from defending their own town. Usually each guild sent so many men, and you can guess how difficult it was to choose the victims, and how men made excuses to get out of it. Those who did not go had to provide wages and food for those who did—salt, fish and bread.

There were dangers not only outside the town, but inside as well. To stop thieves there was a curfew bell every night at dusk, after which all good folk were supposed to be in their own homes. Besides this, the Mayor and Council decreed that there should be good watchmen keeping watch all night in the streets and especially on the gates, to see if anyone tried to slip out or in. The gates were shut at curfew and opened again at sunrise, and between those times the men on the watch had to patrol the streets and guard the gates, challenging anyone they met. If he ran away from them they raised the hue and cry. This meant that every person near enough to hear the cry had to jump out of bed as fast as he could and run after the suspected man. If he didn't go he was fined 6s 8d, and if anyone raised a false hue and cry he was fined 10 shillings.

Sometimes the Town Council had to punish its own members for quarrelling. Do you remember John Halle, the rich wool merchant? He was about as quarrelsome as his chief rival, William Swayne. These two shouted at each other so loudly in the Council meeting that the rest got tired of it. In the Minute Book of the Council we read :

Several meetings having been broken up owing to quarrels . . . it was ordered that whenever the Mayor should convene a meeting, no one of the 24 or the 48 should indulge in personal invective under a penalty of 3s 4d, and if William Swayne or John Halle should again offend in this respect, they are to be fined 20s, and if a second time 40s and if a third time they shall be imprisoned.

Personal invective just means calling the other fellow all the rude names you can think of !

The Council had another way of stopping quarrels. On one occasion they made the man who started the quarrel give a good supper to the Mayor and the twenty-four ; he had to provide a *cygnet*, rabbits, woodcocks, with white wine to drink. So they said : " Let there be an end and let them be good friends." Do you think this was a good way of settling quarrels ?

As you know, the state of the streets in Salisbury was horrible. And yet they did try to do something about this. The Mayor and Council made a great many rules, but you see, they did not have paid roadmen and dustmen as we do and could only appeal to the burgesses themselves to clean and repair the streets. Every burgess was supposed to keep his own bit of pavement and street clean and there was a fine of 40d for not doing this, but I am afraid the fine was not much use ! Sometimes the Council ordered the townsfolk to repair the roads, working often on Sundays. They got bread and ale while they worked, but anyone who did not come was fined 4d. One of the rules the Council made may surprise you. It was that no pigs, geese or ducks were to be allowed to wander in the streets. This seems odd for a town, but you must remember that Salisbury folk had once been country folk and they never quite forgot this. Still, it was a nuisance having livestock in the main streets and the Council tried to stop it. They also said that no one was to throw anything evil-smelling into the streets or the town ditch, and that no animals were to be slaughtered in the roads, only in the proper *shambles*.

The thing the townsfolk of Salisbury dreaded more than anything else was FIRE. When one of the wooden thatched houses in these narrow streets caught fire, the flames might sweep all over the town. But they had no fire engines like ours. As soon as the great bell tolled the fire-alarm, all the folk came tumbling out of their houses to fight it. Here are some people fighting a fire :

Everyone had to provide weapons for fire-fighting. The Council made a rule that each alderman should supply two leather buckets. Besides this, each burgess was supposed to keep a bucket of water handy, and in various parts of the town there were long fire-hooks hanging up which could be used for pulling down burning roofs. Ask your father and mother if these regulations remind them of the last war. The Council tried hard to make people build stone chimneys and tiled roofs, instead of wooden and thatched ones, but you must know how slow people are to change their customs !

You remember that the townsfolk were very anxious to stop cheats and frauds. To stop these the Council made rules that no one should start selling before 9 o'clock, that everything must be sold in the proper place for that kind of article, and that no stranger should sell without getting a licence and paying a fee. They had ' searchers ' to look for bad or deceitful work, and made them take an oath. This is the oath of the searchers in leather :

> You shall swear that you well and truly shall do your office in searching and sealing leather, that it be well and sufficiently tanned, and that being sufficiently tanned you do thereupon set the seal for that purpose to you committed.

You notice that when the goods have been inspected they are sealed or stamped.

As we have seen, there were special rules about cloth and a special inspector called the Aulnager. There were also special rules about brewing ale. In 1464 the Council made these orders :

> First, every brewer is to make a good wholesome brew of sufficient strength, and every flagon of the better ale is to be

sold for 1d, and of the second ale three flagons shall sell for 1d.

Second, there are to be four tasters, one in each *ward*, to taste the ale brewed from time to time in their several wards. And if they find it wanting in soundness or strength or flavour, they shall show it to the mayor, and the *tavern* in which the said ale was found shall be forfeited to the Lord Bishop.

As there were a lot of brewers and taverns in Salisbury, the tasters must have found it hard not to get tipsy !

There were also special rules for bakers and butchers. Every so often the Council fixed the price and size of the loaves of bread. All the loaves had to be sold openly in the market and officials came round to inspect them. If a baker made loaves that were too small or too poor in quality he was fined for the first offence, but if he did it again he had to stand in the *pillory*. One of the great problems then was how to get a standard measure on which everyone agreed. Do you know how we make sure to-day that everyone measures by the same length yard-stick, and that a shopkeeper's pound and ounce weights are exactly right ? If you don't know, try to find out, for this is really a very important thing when you are shopping. In Salisbury it was the searchers' job to check the weights and measures, but even then people felt they wanted a standard to go by, especially for wheat. So in 1485 the Council got a bronze bushel measure,

 called a Winchester measure, which was the proper standard one. Every baker had to check his bushel by this one. It is still in the Salisbury Museum.

Here are some of the rules for butchers :

They must not slaughter their beasts in front of the stalls, but only behind. They must not melt their fat by day because of the smell, only by night. They must not empty their rubbish into the river except at one special place. Foreign butchers (outsiders) must have their stalls in one special place to themselves.

Of course, when the searchers did their job properly they detected all kinds of frauds. These are some of the cases which had to be punished :

John Penrose sold unsound and unwholesome red wine. He was condemned to drink a draught of the same wine and have the rest poured over his head.

John Russell sold 37 pigeons all bad. He had to stand in the pillory and have the pigeons burnt underneath.

John Strode put dust in his bread. When the loaves were broken there was no bread but only strings of cobwebs !

Alice Pegges sold loaves of bread which weighed four-fifths of an ounce too little.

Richard of Walton dyed his cloth with madder and woad instead of with pure woad as he pretended to do.

In the cases where no punishments are given, you can invent appropriate ones yourself !

One of the most important duties of the town was to elect Members of Parliament when the King called them to Westminster. The King had always had a council of great lords to advise him, but in the thirteenth century, a little while after the new Salisbury had been built, he began to think it would be a good idea to have country gentlemen up at Westminster to help him as well as nobles. For one thing, he thought they might give him bigger taxes. He was always short of money and that is probably why he had the brilliant idea of also calling rich merchants from the most important towns to his Parliaments.

It was Edward I who made real use of this idea, and so, in 1294, a royal message came to Salisbury ordering the town to send two burgesses up to his Parliament. Probably no one really wanted to go, for it was a long and dangerous ride up to London, and the townsfolk were a little nervous about what would happen to them when they got there. But Richard Pynnock and John Braundeston were chosen and went up. I do not suppose they had any idea how important these Parliaments would become in the future.

In 1300 when they were again commanded to send members up to Parliament, the Mayor and Aldermen chose six of the best and most discreet men in each ward to meet and choose the members. What do you think of this way of running a Parliamentary election? How does it differ from ours? After that, Salisbury began to send M.Ps. up to London regularly. At first people were not very keen to go, even though the town paid their expenses, for it took them away from their businesses and far too often, when they got there, they found the King chiefly wanted to make them agree to a heavy tax. But after a bit they began to see that it was a very useful thing to go to Parliament for they could help themselves and the town a good deal by bringing their grievances to the House of Commons. Sending M.Ps. to Parliament made Salisbury more important, and gradually they came to see this.

Lastly, the Mayor and Council had to arrange for the town festivities. We have already talked about many of the processions and feasts. For these the Town Council provided the *minstrels*, and so the town had music and dancing whenever it wanted. The Council also looked after the *mummers* and their curious clothes, and arranged for the plays to be acted.

The greatest occasions they had to arrange for were the King's visits to Salisbury. The King had a royal palace close by at Clarendon, and when he came down there to hunt he sometimes visited Salisbury as well. Then the Mayor called out all the townsfolk to ride and meet him and usually there were plays and shows for his entertainment and some presents as well. When King Edward IV and his Queen came in 1466, the Mayor and Aldermen rode out in new robes of scarlet, and all the burgesses were in new green gowns. They collected a present of money for the Queen and also gave her some cattle—a rather curious present! And the Mayor, who was the famous John Halle at that time, opened casks of wine for everyone to drink the King's health.

The Town Council, you see, had a great many matters to deal with. They often had to spend a good deal of money, and this meant, of course, that they had to tax all the burgesses. The money was kept in a strong chest with a very complicated lock that needed three keys to open it. Each of these keys was kept by a different person. Can you see the reason for this? Of course the people wished to make sure that their money was properly spent. So the Council had to present accounts to the burgesses in which they could see how it was all spent. Sometimes a meeting of all the burgesses had to be held. This probably took place in St. Thomas's church. Probably the great bell was rung, or the town-crier went round shouting " Every burgess go to St. Thomas, haste, haste ! " Then they all crowded in to hear the business, and decide on the affairs of their town.

Do you notice what a lot happens in St. Thomas's church ? Besides the ordinary services, there are many guild services there. The new Mayor is elected there and the M.Ps. The burgesses hold all their meetings in church ; lost property and stray sheep are proclaimed there ; the King's proclamations are read, and sometimes they even keep weapons for defending the town there. The church is the centre of all the town life. It belongs to everyone, and all the people give presents to make it more beautiful.

EXCITING TIMES IN SALISBURY

Imagine you are in Salisbury in the summer of 1415. Why are all these dusty soldiers pouring into the town ? Day after day they arrive in bands under their captains, companies of knights on horseback in full armour, foot-soldiers with pikes and archers with bows. It is the King's army assembling for the great war with France which is just about to begin ! All these men are on their way to Southampton where the King is gathering ships to transport the great expedition across the Channel. Henry V has not yet quite decided to make war on France, he is still arguing with the French envoys over a possible peace, but he means to get back what he calls his just possessions in France and so he is preparing for war.

It is a good job these marching bands do not stop long in Salisbury, for the townsfolk dislike them intensely. They always are suspicious of ' foreigners ' and some of these foot-soldiers from the north look such out-landish ruffians that the rich Salisbury burgesses wonder if they will be robbed and murdered in their beds. One Sunday in August, when all the townsfolk are out in the streets enjoying themselves, a band of forty Lancashire men marches up under their captain, Sir James Harrington. Just the other side of Fisherton Bridge they stop to rest. As they sprawl by the road, eating and drinking, up comes a party of Salisbury apprentices, ready for any mischief. They start to poke fun at the foreigners, then one of them in joke tips his tankard of ale all over the head of a fiery-looking warrior. Up he starts, red in the face and furious, and hits out at the Salisbury lad. The apprentices fly to the rescue and half a dozen soldiers hurl themselves into the fray. In an instant there is an uproar. " Alarm ! Alarm ! The town is attacked ! " someone cries, running over the bridge and up the street. The great bell tolls the alarm, the townspeople snatch their knives and daggers, and everyone rushes down Fisherton Street towards the battle. And a fine battle it is too !

The forty Lancastrians are trying to capture the bridge and push into the town, and against them surge the armed townsmen determined to thrust them out. Backwards and forwards the fight sways on the bridge. This is a dangerous place to do battle, for the bridge is narrow, and one after another four men topple over to their death in the river. There is a howl of rage from a fierce little Welshman as one of the Lancastrians snatches his hood and spears it on his pike. The owner is one of the town minstrels and he is just rushing after the enemy with dagger drawn when he is nearly ridden down by a mounted knight who charges furiously into the midst of the scuffle with drawn sword. It is Sir John Harrington. " Back ! Back ! " he yells to his men. " Are you mad to join battle with these paltry townsmen ?

You have other and worthier enemies to fight!" The soldiers disentangle themselves reluctantly, turn round and march away, pursued by stones and howls of rage from the Salisbury people. The town is furious at the insult to its peace, and most angry of all is the little Welsh minstrel at the loss of his good hood. So he follows Sir James, demanding compensation for his loss. Now the King has given a strict order to the captains not to fight English folk, and so Sir James rather grudgingly decides he had better shut this little fellow's mouth. The Welshman comes back triumphantly with 18d for a new hood, and the town begins to settle down again.

But soon bigger events occupy everyone's thoughts. The King summons the town to provide 100 marks towards the cost of his war in France and to send a band of 'archers and other defensible men' to join his army at Southampton. This is bad news for the Mayor and Council and they hold a rather gloomy meeting to think how they can raise the money and the men. Finally they call the heads of all the Guilds together and make them promise so much each. One fine day all the bells are ringing and all the townsfolk crowding the streets to see the Salisbury men marching off to the wars.

Then things begin to get exciting. More troops march through on the Southampton road. King's Messengers  gallop through on urgent business. News comes that the King has reached Southampton, and then, that he has sailed at last! In St. Thomas's the people pray for a fair wind for the fleet. It is an anxious time waiting. Suppose the French retaliate by invading England! There are plenty of French pirate ships in the Channel and only a few years back they raided the south coast. If they landed in force a French army might even reach Salisbury—only 25 miles from the coast. A letter arrives from the King's Council ordering the Mayor and Council to see that Salisbury is well-defended, and everyone expects the invasion. Instead, a messenger gallops in one day from Southampton to announce the tremendous news of King Henry V's great victory at Agincourt.

This is a great day for the town of Salisbury, as it is for London and other towns of England. The bells ring in every church, bonfires are lighted, guild brethren gather for feasting and in all the streets there is dancing and games. The Mayor and Council assemble in solemn state and take out the great Minute Book of the Council. In it they record that on this day came news of the King's great victory over his enemies, the French. By and by the Salisbury men come marching home again and with them comes the song that men are singing about Agincourt.

> Our King went forth to Normandy
> With grace and might of chivalry,
> The God for him wrought marvellously,
> Wherefore England may call and cry
> *Deo gratias, Deo gratias, Anglia,*
> *Redde pro victoria.*

[The last two lines in Latin mean : " England, give thanks to God for victory."]

OLD SARUM: NEW SARUM : NEWER SARUM

Seven hundred years ago, when they moved from Old Sarum, Bishop Poore planned out New Sarum. It was a good plan for those days and probably the streets were quite wide enough for the horses, carts and walkers who went up and down. But to-day Salisbury has grown much bigger, hundreds more people push along the pavements, and the streets are jammed with motor-cars and buses that would give Bishop Poore the shock of his life if he could see them. His streets are much too narrow now and his town too small. So new planners are working on the problem of a plan for NEWER SARUM. They want to make some new roads, to stop buses going along the old narrow streets in the centre (the part Bishop Poore built), and to stop people building any high modern buildings which would hide the beautiful cathedral spire. I wonder if these plans will be carried out as well as Bishop Poore's.

Has your town got a modern town plan ? If so, try to find out what the planners want to do. Discuss the good and bad points of your new town plan together. It would be a good thing to discuss in class the whole idea of town-planning. Do you think people should be allowed to build just where and how they please, so that towns and villages grow up all higgledy-piggledy ? Or do you think Town Councils ought to make plans for houses, streets, factories, etc., and stick to them ? There are probably good and bad points on both sides, but which is really better ?

HOW CAN WE FIND OUT ABOUT PEOPLE IN THE PAST?

Perhaps you are suspicious about all I have been telling you. Perhaps you are saying to yourself: " How does she know? I believe she is making it all up! " I assure you I have not invented anything—only used a little imagination on the clues I found. To find out how people lived in the past you have to use every clue you can get. Here is a list of all I used for Salisbury.

1. *What I could see with my own eyes :*
    The chalk downs, the rivers and the water-meadows (*i.e.* the geographical position of Salisbury).
    The ramparts of Old Sarum, the cathedral and the churches.
    Old houses in Salisbury.
    The gates and walls, the plan and the names of the streets.
    Furniture and other old things (like the Giant) in the Museum.

2. *What I could see in old pictures, especially pictures which people in the fifteenth century drew themselves :*
    Many of the pictures in this book are drawn from these old pictures.

3. *What I could read that the people of the past wrote themselves. For example :*
    the letter that the clergy wrote to the Pope ;
    the charter which the King gave to Salisbury ;
    the books written by the Guilds ;
    the rules made by the Town Council ;
    the account books kept by the Town Council ;
    inscriptions in the churches ;
    the wills people made before they died ;
    records kept in the King's law courts.

If you want to find out about your own town you can use the same sort of clues.

1. Find out all you can by *looking carefully round about you.* It is surprising how blind we can be until we really start to look properly !

Look at the geographical picture of your town and the country round it : is it on a hill, by a river, in a valley ?

Look at old churches and houses : have any got dates on them ?

Look at anything else that is old—a castle, abbey, almshouses.

Look at street names : do they tell you anything about the town's past ?

2. Find out all you can by visiting your local museum, if you have one.

3. Get books about your town from the public library and look at any old pictures or photographs. Notice carefully the date at which these pictures were made. What do they tell you ? You might collect old photographs yourself.

4. Ask your teacher to help you find out if you can still see some of the things people of the past wrote, like letters, diaries, wills, account books, chronicles of what happened. You will probably need someone to help you read them.

5. Ask if your town has a charter or any old records of how it was governed, or how its Guilds managed their affairs.

Perhaps you could make a book about your own town (or village).

THINGS TO DO

HOW TOWNS BEGAN

1. How many places can you find near your home with names ending in *ton* ?

2. Look at a map of England and pick out five towns which you think were built for any of the reasons given on page 3.

3. Get a map of your county and pick out places which grew up round a castle, cathedral or monastery.

4. What about your own town—if you live in one? Do you know why it is just where it is? Ask for a history of it and find out when it began and why. Has it got a charter? If so, ask to see it.

5. Can you find the foundation stone of your own parish church?

6. How many yards are there in a perch? See if you can measure out in your playground the plot of ground (7 perches by 3) each Salisbury burgess had. Is it larger or smaller than the area of your home?

7. Make a list of trades at which people work in your town or village. Compare it with the Salisbury list on page 10. What trades on your list would you *not* have found in Salisbury 500 years ago?

CATHEDRAL BUILDERS

1. Collect pictures of English cathedrals. Compare them carefully with the pictures of Salisbury and try to decide where they are alike and where different in style (*e.g.* are the windows round or pointed at the top?)

2. Salisbury is in the *Early English* style. Make drawings of windows, pillars, arches, doors, etc., to guide you in recognizing the same style in other churches. Can you find out about the *Norman* style (which comes before) and the *Perpendicular* (which comes after)?

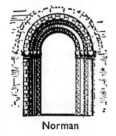  

Norman   Early English   Perpendicular

3. Visit any churches near you which were built before 1500. Decide which parts are Norman, or Early English or Perpendicular in style.

4. Learn the correct names for the different parts of a church (nave, choir, etc.) from the plan of Salisbury cathedral on page 15. Then make a plan of your own parish church and put in all the correct names (but your church will probably not have two transepts).

MARKETS AND SHOPS

1. Have you a market in your own town? When is it held? Can you find out when it began? Make a list of all the different things sold there to-day and compare it with what was sold in Salisbury in the fifteenth century. If you have not got a market, take any shop and make a list of what is sold there. How many of these things would you not have found in Salisbury 500 years ago?

2. Pick out in the plan on page 8 all the various places where different kinds of goods were sold. Do you know any other old town where the street names show what used to be sold there?

3. Collect as many different pictures as you can of things made in the fifteenth century, e.g. carved chests, stools, pottery, pewter. Or if you have a museum, go and look for fifteenth-century things and draw them.

4. Write the conversation between the man and woman on page 29 as we should say it to-day. Can you paint a picture of the man buying mulberry cloth?

5. Discuss together in class :
    (a) Would it be a good thing to stop strangers coming to live or trade in your town?
    (b) Would it be a good idea to go back to the plan of making everyone who sells the same goods have their shops in one street?
    (c) Why was there no Woolworths in fifteenth-century Salisbury?

(*d*) Why were goods from abroad so dear in the fifteenth century ? Find out why to-day we have so many things from abroad which are quite cheap—*e.g.* oranges, rice, tea.

CLOTHES

1. Make a frieze for your classroom of fifteenth-century people in their proper dress.

2. Collect pictures of fifteenth-century fashions and modern ones. Put them side by side and compare them. Perhaps you may come across a modern fashion which has been copied from a fifteenth-century one.

3. Discuss these questions : Do you think the fifteenth-century fashions are better or worse than ours ? Do you like the idea of bright colours for men's clothes ?

STREETS AND WALLS

1. (*a*) What is done with the rubbish from your town ?
(*b*) Where does your water come from ?

2. The Mayor of Salisbury got permission to dig a ditch round the town because of robbers. How are we protected from them to-day ? Why is it much more difficult for thieves to escape in a town to-day ?

3. Do you know any towns in England that still have old walls or gates ? If you can, make a collection in your class of picture postcards or drawings of these.

HOUSES AND FURNITURE

1. Make a list of all the things that have to be done to-day in building a house. How many on your list would not have been done in the fifteenth century ? Why ?

2. Collect pictures of fifteenth-century houses and furniture.

3. Have you ever made a list or inventory of all the furniture in your house ? A wine-merchant, named Hugh le Bevere, once did this. On the next page is his list.

6 casks of wine and a funnel.

1 table, 4 table-cloths and 2 chairs.

A bowl called a mazer, made of maplewood.

A cocoanut-shell cup in a silver stand and with a silver cover.

6 silver spoons.

1 cupboard, 6 chests and 2 coffers.

1 mattress, 3 feather-beds, 7 linen sheets, 2 pillows.

6 blankets and 1 torn counterpane.

1 green carpet for the table.

2 curtains, 5 cushions, 1 candlestick and 1 grate.

1 spit, 1 frying-pan, 1 big brass pot and 3 small ones.

4 little pots, 2 basins, 1 metal plate, 1 brass plate.

1 quilted jacket and 1 iron helmet.

Study this list carefully. (Do you notice the carpet is on the *table*?) What have you got in your house that Hugh had not? Why do you think he needed a jacket and helmet for war?

4. What makes your house more comfortable than a fifteenth-century one?

5. Paint a picture of the hall in Richard Gilbert's house (see page 43).

FOOD

Make a menu of your own meals for one day and compare what you have to eat with fifteenth-century meals (pages 22, 52 and 62).

PEOPLE AT WORK

1. Find out all you can about trade unions. Then make a list of all the differences between trade unions and guilds.

2. Do you think the guilds were a good idea? Could you run your class as a guild? (Remember that *all* have to be in it.) Make some guild rules for the class.

3. Do we try to stop bad workmanship to-day? If so, how?

PEOPLE AT PLAY

1. Make a set of drawings of present-day amusements to match the set of fifteenth-century amusements on page 65.

2. Find out in your own town or village whether any people of the past helped to build and beautify the church or gave money

to hospitals, schools, almshouses, etc. Has anyone recently made any gifts to the town ?

3. Paint a picture of a guild procession.

4. Hold a debate on whether people of the fifteenth century enjoyed themselves more or less than we do.

5. Write and act a play about St. George and the dragon.

TOWN GOVERNMENT

1. If you live in a town, find out the name of the Councillor for your ward. Perhaps he would tell you what he has to do. Try to arrange a visit to a Town Council meeting. If you live in the country, find out who looks after your school, your roads and your village hall.

2. What happens when a fire breaks out in your town or village ?

3. Can you find out what safety rules are enforced in your nearest cinema ?

4. Find out how many different kinds of inspector are employed round you. What things are inspected now which would not have been in the fifteenth century ? What things were inspected in those days which are not inspected to-day ?

5. Write and act a scene in a Town Council meeting 500 years ago. (You could have a real good quarrel between two burgesses, as they did in Salisbury—see page 69.)

EXCITING TIMES

1. Tell the story of the victory of Agincourt as if you were one of the soldiers come back to your town.

2. Find out if any exciting events happened in your town in the past, *e.g.* battles, visits of kings, a great fire. How do we know about these exciting events of the past to-day ?

3. Has anything happened lately in your town or village that ought to be remembered in days to come ? How will people in a hundred years' time know about *our* doings unless we write them down ? So why not start a diary of exciting times in your own town ? Perhaps hundreds of years later someone will read it.

GLOSSARY

This is a list of special words. If the word you want to know is not here, look for it in your dictionary.

aniseed : seed of a plant called anise, used in cooking and in medicines.

architect : man who plans buildings.

aulnager : inspector who sees that cloth is up to the proper standard.

burgess : man who is a full member of the town community with all its rights and duties.

buttery : larder for bread, ale, butter, etc.

canons : cathedral clergy.

capon : cock for eating.

chapter : meeting of cathedral clergy.

chapter-house : place where they meet.

charter : written document solemnly promising rights, etc., to those to whom it is given.

chorister : choir boy.

cloisters : covered walk, usually round a square of grass.

close : space round a cathedral which belongs to the Church.

curfew : bell rung at a fixed time in the evening.

cygnet : a young swan.

ell : measure for cloth, etc. (45 inches).

fuller : man who ' finished ' cloth by beating it in water.

fustian : thick, rough cloth.

haberdashery : small articles to do with clothes, *e.g.* cotton, needles, pins.

hose : stockings.

kerchief : cloth to put on the head or round the neck.

knuckle-bones : a game played with small bones or stones.

Lady Chapel : part of a church specially dedicated to the Mother of Jesus Christ.

livery : special uniform of a guild, armed band, etc.

mason : man who cuts stones and builds with them.

mazer : large cup or bowl with a lid.

mead : drink made from fermented honey and water.

miniver : fur used for special ceremonies, *e.g.* knighting a nobleman.

minstrel : man who sings and plays a musical instrument.

morris dance : old dance for which the dancers dress up in various costumes.

mummer : actor disguised in strange costume, often with animal head.

nave : main part of a church where the congregation usually sits.

packhorse : horse used to carry packs or bundles of goods.

palisade : fence made of pointed sticks.

parchment : skin, especially of goat or sheep, scraped smooth for writing on.

pedlar : man who travels round with goods for sale.

perch : measure of length equal to $5\frac{1}{2}$ yards.

pewter : mixture of tin, lead, sometimes copper, used to make plates, mugs, etc.

pewterer : man who makes pewter articles.

piccage : fee paid by a stranger for permission to set up his stall and sell in the market.

pillory : wooden frame with holes through which the head and hands of a criminal were pushed.

points : laces with tags (like shoe-laces) used to keep stockings up, or to lace up a doublet.

rampart : bank of earth thrown up to defend or fortify a place.

russet : reddish-brown.

sable : brown or black fur.

saffron : crocus flower used for flavouring cakes or colouring them yellow.

shambles : place where butchers kill animals.

sumptuary laws : laws telling people what kind of clothes they might or might not wear.

surcoat : loose robe worn on top of armour.

tavern : inn.

taverner : inn-keeper.

tenter : frame on which cloth is stretched and dried.

tenter-ground : place where the tenters are put.

tiler : man who makes tiles.

toll-taker : man who collects tolls or fees from people.

transept : part of a church.

vat : large tank.

venison : meat of deer.

vintner : man who sells wine.

ward : part (or sub-division) of a town.

wattle hurdles : bundles made of a thin wooden lattice-work.